Made in the USA
Columbia, SC
27 February 2023

13038660R00067